The Quarantine Cookbook

50 Best Recipes for Successful Self-Isolation

BY

Christina Tosch

Table of Contents

Introduction

Regardless of whether you are self-isolating for safety's sake or quarantined because you aren't feeling well, there are plenty of ways to make hearty, healthy meals. Better yet, to be successful, you don't need to have lots of special ingredients to hand either.

It's time to put that extra time you are spending self-isolating or in quarantine to good use. The Quarantine Cookbook will show you that home cooking is a great way to keep your hands busy and your mind motivated during these trying times!

With some ingredients proving more difficult to source, basic and canned foods are becoming increasingly popular.

These 50 recipes for self-isolation and quarantine include main meals featuring everything you need to stay healthy, including fruit, veggies, pulses, grains, pasta, and rice.

What's more, every one of these recipes for successful self-isolation and quarantine makes use of ingredients that are most likely hidden in the back of your kitchen cupboards!

Home cooking during self-isolation and quarantine can be fun and therapeutic; recipes needn't take too many ingredients, be expensive, or take too much time.

Pasta Noodle Dishes

Artichoke Florentine Pasta

Nobody could guess that this sophisticated-tasting pasta dish starts with canned artichokes!

Servings: 8

Total Time: 35mins

Ingredients:

- 1 pound penne pasta
- 6 tbsp butter
- 4 garlic cloves (peeled and minced)
- 16 cups fresh baby spinach
- ¼ cup all-purpose flour
- 3 cups skim milk
- 8 ounces cream cheese
- ¾ cup Parmesan cheese (grated)
- 1 tsp salt
- ½ tsp black pepper
- ¼ tsp cayenne pepper
- ½ cup dry white wine
- 2 (14 ounces) cans water-packed artichoke hearts (drained, chopped)
- ⅓ cup Italian-style breadcrumbs

Directions:

1. First, cook the penne according to the packet instructions and until al dente.

2. In the meantime, melt 2 tablespoons of butter in a Dutch oven over moderately high heat.

3. Add the garlic to the pan, then sauté for 30 seconds. Next, add the spinach and stir for 1-2 minutes until just wilted. Take out of the pan and set to one side.

4. Using the same Dutch oven, melt the remaining butter over moderately high heat.

5. Whisk in the flour until smooth. While whisking, pour in the milk. Bring the mixture to a boil. Then, cook for 2-3 minutes while stirring continuously until the mixture has thickened.

6. To the pot, add the cream cheese, Parmesan cheese, salt, black pepper, cayenne pepper, and white wine and stir to combine.

7. Stir in the chopped artichokes, cook until hot through.

8. Next, drain the cooked pasta and add to the Dutch oven. Toss to combine.

9. Fold in the set-aside spinach.

10. Divide the pasta between serving bowls. Then, garnish each portion with a sprinkling of breadcrumbs.

11. Serve straight away.

Baked Spaghetti

Delicate angel hair spaghetti is tossed with a rich beef sauce and topped with three kinds of melting cheese – yummy! This dish is one that kids will enjoy too.

Servings: 6

Total Time: 45mins

Ingredients:

- Butter (to grease)
- 1 (14½ ounces) can diced tomatoes
- 1 (8 ounces) can tomato sauce
- 1 cup water
- 1 chicken bouillon cube
- 1 tsp vinegar
- 1 tsp Worcestershire sauce
- ¼ cup fresh parsley (chopped)
- 2 cloves garlic (peeled and minced)
- 1 tsp powdered garlic
- 1 tbsp Italian seasoning
- 1 tbsp granulated sugar
- 1 bay leaf
- 1 cup ground beef (cooked)
- 8 ounces angel hair pasta
- 1 cup Cheddar cheese (shredded)
- 1 cup mozzarella cheese (shredded)
- 4 ounces cream cheese (cubed and softened)

Directions:

1. First, preheat the main oven to 350 degrees F. Grease a square 8" dish with butter.

2. Combine the canned tomatoes, tomato sauce, water, bouillon cube, vinegar, Worcestershire sauce, parsley, garlic, powdered garlic, Italian seasoning, granulated sugar, and bay leaf in a saucepan over moderately high heat. Then, bring the mixture to a boil. Turn down to a simmer approximately for 20 minutes.

3. Stir in the ground beef and cook for 5 more minutes.

4. Next, in the meantime, cook the angel hair pasta in boiling water for 60 seconds less than the packet instructs. When your pasta is cooked, drain away the water. Then, toss the pasta with ½ cup Cheddar cheese, ½ cup mozzarella, 2 ounces of the cream cheese.

5. Discard the bay leaf from the meat sauce, pour the meat sauce over the pasta and toss to combine.

6. Next, transfer the mixture to your prepared baking dish. Scatter the remaining Cheddar and mozzarella over the pasta.

7. Dot the remaining cubes of cream cheese on top of the pasta.

8. Bake in the oven for half an hour until the cheese has melted. Allow to rest for 2-3 minutes before serving.

Canned Salmon Fettuccine

Say goodbye to canned salmon and cucumber sandwiches, and instead use this tinned fish to create a creamy fettuccine main meal for six.

Servings: 6

Total Time: 20mins

Ingredients:

- 3 tbsp butter
- 1 tsp garlic (peeled and minced)
- 1 (12 ounces) can fat-free evaporated milk
- 18-24 ounces fettuccine
- 1 cup Parmesan cheese (shredded)
- ½ tsp sea salt
- ¼ tsp ground black pepper
- 1 (4 ounces) can mushrooms (drained)
- 1 (15 ounces) can sweet peas (drained)
- 1 (5 ounces) can skinless, boneless pink salmon (broken up)

Directions:

1. First, in a skillet, melt the butter and add the garlic. Cook for 60 seconds before pouring in the evaporated milk and bringing it to a simmer.

2. Next, in your large pot of boiling water, cook the fettuccine until al dente. Drain and keep warm.

3. Whisk the shredded cheese into the pan containing the garlic butter and season with salt and pepper. Continue to simmer while the pasta cooks.

4. When the pasta is cooked, add the mushrooms, peas, and cooked fettuccine to the cheese mixture and toss to evenly coat. Fold in the canned salmon.

Creamy Turkey Noodle Soup

This hearty soup is thick, creamy, and comforting. It's the perfect pick-me-up if you're feeling a little stressed and overwhelmed with everything going on in the outside world.

Servings: 8

Total Time: 30mins

Ingredients:

- ⅓ cup butter (cubed)
- 1 rib celery (diced)
- 1 carrot (shredded)
- ⅓ cup all-purpose flour
- 1 (32 ounces) carton chicken broth
- ½ cup skim milk
- ½ cup half half
- 1 cup uncooked egg noodles
- 2 cups cooked turkey (cubed)
- 1½ cups Cheddar cheese (shredded)
- ¼ tsp salt
- ¼ tsp black pepper

Directions:

1. Melt the butter in your saucepan over moderately high heat firstly, add the celery and carrot and sauté for 3-5 minutes until tender.

2. Whisk in the flour until incorporated.

3. Pour in the broth, milk, and half half.

4. Next, bring the mixture to a boil while stirring continually for 3-4 minutes.

5. Stir in the egg noodles. Turn the heat down to a simmer. Then, cook for 8-10 minutes until the noodles are al dente.

6. Stir in the turkey, shredded cheese, salt, and black pepper. Continue to cook until then the mixture is hot through and the cheese has melted.

7. Serve.

Macaroni Chicken Salad with Pineapple and Raisins

Fresh and fruity, this chicken pasta salad will lift everyone's spirits.

Servings: 2

Total Time: 25mins

Ingredients:

- 8 ounces cooked, leftover, or rotisserie chicken (chopped)
- ½ cup white onion (peeled and chopped small)
- ½ cup celery (chopped)
- ½ cup store-bought sweet pickle relish
- ½ cup raisins
- ¾ cup mayonnaise
- ½ cup sour cream
- 2 cups cooked elbow pasta
- 1 tsp salt
- 1 tsp white pepper
- ¾ cup canned pineapple bits or small chunks (drained)

Directions:

1. In a bowl, combine the chopped chicken with the onion, celery, relish, and raisins.

2. Stir in the mayonnaise and sour cream and combine.

3. Cover the bowl with a lid and place in the fridge until ready to use.

4. Once the pasta is entirely cool, add the chicken salad mixture. Stir well to combine—season to taste with salt and white pepper and fold in the chunks of pineapple.

5. Serve at once.

One-Pot Bacon Cheeseburger Pasta

Save on the washing-up with this one-pot bacon cheeseburger pasta that the whole family can share.

Servings: 6

Total Time: 35mins

Ingredients

- 4 bacon slices (chopped)
- 1 pound ground beef
- 1 small red onion (peeled and chopped)
- 6 ounces uncooked spiral pasta
- 2 cups chicken broth
- 1 (14½ ounces) can crushed tomatoes
- ½ (8 ounce) can tomato sauce
- ½ cup water
- 2 tbsp ketchup
- 1½ tbsp prepared Dijon mustard
- 1 tbsp Worcestershire sauce
- Pinch of salt
- Dash of black pepper
- 1 cup Cheddar cheese (freshly shredded)
- 2 ¾ tbsp chopped dill pickle
- To Serve (Optional):
- Tomatoes (chopped)
- Lettuce (shredded)
- Sliced dill pickles
- Red onion (peeled and sliced)

Directions:

1. In a stockpot of 3-4 quart capacity over moderate heat, cook the bacon while occasionally stirring for 6-8 minutes, until crisp. Using your slotted spoon, remove the bacon from the pan and set aside on kitchen paper towels. Discard the fat drippings.

2. Using the same pan over moderate heat, cook the beef and onion while breaking the beef up using the back of a spoon, for 6-8 minutes until the meat is no longer pink.

3. Add the pasta, broth, tomatoes, tomato sauce, water, ketchup, mustard, Worcestershire sauce, salt, and black pepper. Turn the heat down, cover with a lid and simmer for 8-10 minutes, until the pasta is al dente.

4. Stir in half of the Cheddar, followed by the chopped dill pickle and bacon.

5. Serve the pasta with the remaining Cheddar and your preferred choice of extras.

Orzo Turkey Burgers

Orzo is more substantial than rice but less bulky than regular pasta and combined with lean ground turkey to create patties; it's a healthy choice for your whole family.

Servings: 4

Total Time: 25mins

Ingredients:

- 1 cup panko breadcrumbs

- 1 cup cottage cheese

- ½ pound 99% lean ground turkey

- 4 ounces canned mushrooms (drained, chopped and patted dry)

- 1 tsp Italian seasoning

- 1 tbsp olive oil (divided)

- ½ cup orzo pasta

- 1 cup store-bought pasta sauce (of choice)

Directions:

1. Cook, drain, but do not rinse the orzo as per the package instructions.

2. In the meantime, through a fine-mesh strainer, strain the cottage cheese into a bowl.

3. Lightly shake the strainer to drain.

4. In a second bowl, add the cooked orzo pasta to the cottage cheese and mushrooms followed by the ground turkey and Italian seasoning.

5. When the mixture is incorporated, shape it into 8 (½") thick patties.

6. Add the breadcrumbs to a shallow pan.

7. Coat each patty on both sides in the crumbs.

8. In a 10" nonstick frying pan, over moderate heat, heat ½ tablespoonful of olive oil

9. Cook 4 of the patties for 8-9 minutes, flipping them over halfway through the cooking process until they register an internal heat of 160 degrees F on a meat thermometer.

10. Repeat the process with the remaining patties.

11. Serve with store-bought pasta sauce.

Pasta Puttanesca

Not sure what to do with that can of black olives leftover from the holidays? No problem whip up this quick, one-pan pasta dish using these simple ingredients.

Servings: 4

Total Time: 25mins

Ingredients:

- 12 ounces spaghetti
- 1 tbsp olive oil
- 1 onion (peeled and sliced)
- 2 garlic cloves (peeled and sliced)
- 1 (14 ounces) can chopped tomatoes
- 1 (10½ ounces) can pitted black olives
- 1 (1¾ ounces) canned anchovies
- ½ tsp dried chili flakes
- 1 tbsp capers (roughly chopped)
- Handful fresh parsley (roughly chopped)

Directions:

1. First, in a pan of boiling salted water cook the spaghetti as per the package instructions, and until al dente. Drain.

2. In the meantime, while the pasta cooks, in a large-size skillet or frying pan, heat the oil.

3. Add the onion to the pan and over moderate heat, sauté until softened, for 4-5 minutes.

4. Next, add the garlic. Then, cook for an additional 60 seconds.

5. Add the canned tomatoes along with the black olive and anchovies, chili, and capers. Cook for 5 minutes.

6. Combine the drained pasta with the tomato-caper mixture, garnish with chopped parsley and enjoy.

Pasta with Creamy Chicken and Peaches

Canned peaches are the star of the show in this creamy dish. So, break open a can today and serve this perfect pasta.

Servings: 4

Total Time: 35mins

Ingredients:

- 1 pound lean chicken (cut into strips)
- Salt and black pepper (to season)
- Paprika (to season)
- Italian seasoning (to season)
- 12-14 ounces pasta spirals
- Splash of olive oil
- 1 onion (peeled and finely chopped)
- 1 garlic clove (peeled and crushed)
- 5 ounces cream
- ½ bouillon cube
- 1 zucchini (sliced)
- 7 ounces frozen peas
- 4 canned peach halves (drained)
- 5¼ ounces cream cheese (room temperature)

Directions:

1. Season the chicken strips with salt, pepper, paprika, and Italian seasoning.

2. Cook the pasta spirals in a pan of boiling salted water until al dente. Drain and keep warm.

3. Heat then a splash of olive oil in a frying pan, and add onion and garlic, sauté for few minutes until softened.

4. Add the seasoned chicken and cook for 4-5 minutes on each side until golden and no pink remains.

5. While continually stirring, fold in the cream to incorporate.

6. Next, crumble in the bouillon cube followed by the zucchini and peas and while stirring cook for 5 minutes until heated and cooked through.

7. Add the peaches and cream cheese to the pan and stir until combined and creamy.

8. Lastly, serve the chicken and sauce over the pasta spirals.

Peanut Coated Chicken and Noodle Salad

Buckwheat noodles and tender chicken are tossed in a nutty lime sauce. Fresh red chili gives this tasty salad a spicy kick!

Servings: 4

Total Time: 30mins

Ingredients:

- 5 ounces unsalted roasted peanuts
- 4 skinless, chicken breasts (halved lengthwise)
- 1 egg (lightly beaten)
- 3 ounces dried soba or buckwheat noodles
- 1 cucumber (halved and sliced)
- A small bunch of mint (picked over, large leaves chopped)
- Zest and freshly squeezed juice of 2 limes
- 1-2 tsp sugar
- 1 red chili (seeded and finely sliced)

Directions:

1. First, preheat the main oven to 395 degrees F. Using foil cover a baking tray.

2. Second, add the peanuts to a food processor and finely chop to large –size crumbs, not dust.

3. Place the nuts on a shallow dish.

4. Next, dip the chicken first in the beaten egg. Then, coat on both sides in the chopped peanuts.

5. Place the coated chicken on your baking tray and bake for 15-20 minutes until sufficiently cooked through and golden.

6. Next, in the meantime, cook the noodles according to the package directions. Drain well and rinse under cold running water until cooled and drain once more.

7. When the chicken is cooked, using tongs, or forks, combine the noodles with the cucumber slices, mint, fresh lime juice, lime zest, sugar, and red chili. Taste and season.

8. Serve the noodle salad with the peanut chicken.

Ravioli Lasagna

Dig that ravioli out of the back of the freezer and turn it into a deliciously rich and meaty, oven-baked family-size lasagna.

Servings: 6

Total Time: 1hour 5mins

Ingredients:

- Butter (to grease)
- 1 pound ground beef
- 1 (28 ounces) jar spaghetti sauce
- 1 (25 ounces) package frozen ravioli
- 1½ cups mozzarella cheese (shredded)

Directions:

1. First, preheat the main oven to 400 degrees F. Grease a 2½-quart baking dish.

2. In a skillet over moderate heat, sauté the ground beef until browned all over. Drain any grease from the skillet.

3. Spoon a third of the spaghetti sauce into the base of the baking dish and smooth into an even layer. Then, arrange half of the ravioli on top of the sauce in an even layer and spoon over half of the beef followed by ½ a cup of mozzarella.

4. Repeat these layers one more time.

5. Pour the remaining sauce over lasagna and sprinkle over the remaining cheese.

6. Cover the dish with kitchen foil and bake in the oven for 40-45 minutes, the cheese should be melted and the sauce bubbling.

7. Lastly, allow to rest for 5 minutes before serving.

Salisbury Steak with Egg Noodles

This classic Salisbury Steak dish is the food equivalent of a nice, warm hug, just what's needed in stressful times.

Servings: 6

Total Time: 35mins

Ingredients:

- 1 egg (beaten)
- 1 (10½ ounces) can condensed French onion soup
- ½ cup dry breadcrumbs
- ¼ tsp salt
- Pinch black pepper
- 1½ pounds ground beef
- 1 tbsp all-purpose flour
- ¼ cup water
- ¼ cup tomato ketchup
- ½ tsp mustard
- 1 tsp Worcestershire sauce
- 6 cups cooked egg noodles (hot)

Directions:

1. Combine the beaten egg with a ⅓ of the canned soup along with the breadcrumbs, salt, and black pepper in a bowl.

2. Next, stir in the ground beef. Shape the mixture into 6 equally-sized, oval-shaped patties.

3. In a skillet over moderate heat, brown the patties for 3-4 minutes on each side. Take out of the pan and set to one side.

4. In the same skillet, whisk together the flour and water until smooth. Next, whisk in the tomato ketchup, mustard, Worcestershire sauce, and remaining French onion soup. Bring then the mixture to a boil while stirring for 2 minutes.

5. Return the patties to the skillet, cover with a lid and simmer for 15 minutes or until cooked through.

6. Serve the Salisbury steaks and gravy over cooked egg noodles.

Sausage Stroganoff with Egg Noodles

Are you looking for more budget-friendly meals to help get you through your self-isolation period? Then, this Stroganoff recipe, which calls for tasty sausage instead of more expensive beef, is a great start.

Servings: 4

Total Time: 30mins

Ingredients:

- 8 ounces uncooked wide egg noodles
- 1 pound bulk pork sausage
- 1 yellow onion (peeled, diced)
- 8 ounces fresh mushrooms (sliced)
- 2 cloves of garlic (peeled and minced)
- ¼ cup all-purpose flour
- ¼ tsp paprika
- ¼ tsp salt
- 1½ cups beef broth
- 1 cup sour cream
- Fresh parsley (chopped)

Directions:

1. Cook the noodles using packet instructions. Drain the cooked noodles and set them to one side.

2. In a skillet over moderate heat, sauté the sausage, onion, mushrooms, and garlic for several minutes until the sausage is browned all over.

3. Stir in the flour, paprika, and salt until combined.

4. Next, pour in the broth and stir to combine.

5. Bring the mixture to a boil and cook for 1-2 minutes stirring continually until the liquid thickens.

6. Take the pan off the heat. Then, fold in the sour cream.

7. Garnish with fresh parsley and serve with the cooked noodles.

Sour Cream Noodle Bake

Sometimes the simplest recipe tastes the best, and this easy to prepare noodle bake will feed a family of six without breaking the bank.

Servings: 6

Total Time: 50mins

Ingredients:

- 1 pound ground beef
- ½ yellow onion (peeled and diced)
- 1 clove garlic (peeled and minced)
- 1 (14½ ounces) can tomato sauce
- 12 ounces egg noodles
- ½ cup sour cream
- 1 ¼ cups small curd cottage cheese
- ½ tsp onion powder
- ¼ tsp black pepper
- 1½ cups mature Cheddar cheese (grated)

Directions:

1. First, preheat the main oven to 350 degrees F.

2. Over moderate to high heat, heat a large frying pan.

3. Add the beef along with the onion and cook for 5-8 minutes, until the beef is nearly browned all over and the onions are starting are softened.

4. Next, add the garlic and cook while frequently stirring for 1-2 minutes.

5. Pour in the can of tomato sauce and stir to blend, while simmering.

6. In the meantime, while the ingredients simmer, bring a large pan of water to boil.

7. Add the noodles to the pan. Then, cook until al dente. Drain thoroughly and put to one side.

8. In a mixing bowl, stir the sour cream with the cottage cheese, onion powder, and black pepper until incorporated. Fold the mixture into the noodles to coat evenly and well.

9. Transfer half of the noodle mixture to a 13x9"casserole dish. Then, top with half of the meat sauce and garnish with half of the grated Cheddar. Repeat the layers once more.

10. Next, bake in the oven for 18-20 minutes, or until the cheese is entirely melted.

11. Remove from the oven and allow the bake to rest for a few minutes before serving.

Southern Mac 'n Cheese

Elevate a simple Mac 'n Cheese with the help of some punchy Southern seasonings and tasty Cheddar cheese.

Servings: 6

Total Time: 1hour 5mins

Ingredients:

- Nonstick cooking spray
- 16 ounces macaroni pasta
- 1½ cups whole milk
- ½ cup heavy cream
- 2 eggs (beaten)
- 1 tsp salt
- ½ tsp black pepper
- ½ tsp onion granules
- ¼ tsp powdered garlic
- 8 ounces American cheese (shredded)
- 4 cups Cheddar cheese (shredded)
- 1 tbsp fresh parsley (chopped)

Directions:

1. First, preheat the main oven to 350 degrees F. Spritz a 3-quart baking dish with nonstick cooking spray.

2. Cook the macaroni in boiling water for 60 seconds less than the packet instructs.

3. In a bowl, combine the milk, cream, eggs, salt, black pepper, onion granules, powdered garlic, American cheese, and 3 cups Cheddar.

4. Drain the cooked macaroni. Then, add to the bowl with the other ingredients. Toss to combine.

5. Next, transfer the mixture to the prepared baking dish and cover with kitchen foil.

6. Placed in the oven and bake for 25 minutes. Then, remove the foil and sprinkle over the remaining Cheddar cheese. Bake for another approximately 20 minutes until the cheese melts.

7. Allow to rest for 10 minutes before garnishing with parsley and serving.

Spaghetti with Fried Eggs

Yes really! Although they may not be the most obvious ingredients to pair together well, the result is a deliciously homey dish you'll want to make time and time again.

Servings: 2-3

Total Time: 20mins

Ingredients:

- Salt
- ½ pound angel hair spaghetti
- 6 tbsp extra virgin olive oil
- 2 cloves of garlic (peeled and smashed)
- 4 eggs (lightly beaten)
- Black pepper
- Parmesan cheese (freshly grated, to serve)

Directions:

1. First, bring a deep pot of salted water to a boil and add the angel hair spaghetti, cook using packet instructions.

2. In the meantime, warm 4 tablespoon of the oil in a small skillet over moderately low heat. Add the garlic and sauté until just colored and fragrant. Transfer the contents of the skillet to a bowl and set to one side.

3. Next, add the remaining oil to the same skillet and return to the heat. Fry the 4 eggs in the skillet until the white is set, but the eggs are runny.

4. Drain the pasta. Then, toss it with the eggs—season with black pepper and divide between serving bowls.

5. Garnish with grated Parmesan and enjoy straight away.

Taco Baked Noodles

Transform dinner time into a fiesta with this Mexican-inspired taco noodle dish, the tastiest way to brighten up a boring day.

Servings: 6

Total Time: 35mins

Ingredients:

- Nonstick cooking spray
- 3 cups uncooked wide egg noodles
- 2 pounds lean ground turkey
- 1 sachet taco seasoning
- 1 tsp chili powder
- 1 tsp onion granules
- ½ tsp powdered garlic
- 1 (8 ounces) can tomato sauce
- ½ cup water
- 1 (4 ounces) diced green chilies)
- 1 cup Cheddar cheese (shredded)

Topping:

- 2 cups lettuce (shredded)
- ⅓ cup pitted black olives (sliced)
- 2 tomatoes (chopped)
- ½ cup taco sauce
- ½ cup sour cream

Directions:

1. First, preheat the main oven to 350 degrees F. Spritz a 7x11" baking dish with nonstick cooking spray.

2. Cook the noodles using packet instructions. Drain and set to one side for a moment.

3. In a skillet over moderately high heat, sauté the turkey for several minutes until browned. Drain any fat from the pan.

4. Add the taco seasoning, chili powder, onion granules, powdered garlic, tomato sauce, water, and chilis to the skillet. Stir to combine. Turn the heat down to a simmer. Then, cook for 5 minutes without a lid.

5. Add the cooked noodles to the prepared baking dish in an even layer. Spoon the turkey mixture over the noodles. Sprinkle over the Cheddar cheese.

6. Next, place the baking dish in your oven and bake for 10-15 minutes, until the cheese has melted.

7. Lastly, take the dish out of the oven and top with shredded lettuce, black olives, chopped tomatoes, and taco sauce. Drizzle over the sour cream and serve.

Tortellini Carbonara

This recipe doesn't call for eggs, unlike most other Carbonara recipes, making it a perfect beginner dish that is actually impossible to get wrong!

Servings: 4

Total Time: 25mins

Ingredients:

- 9 ounces chilled cheese tortellini
- 8 rashers bacon (chopped)
- 1 cup heavy whipping cream
- ½ cup Parmesan cheese (grated)
- ½ cup fresh parsley (chopped)

Directions:

1. Cook the tortellini using packet instructions.

2. Next, in the meantime, cook the bacon in a skillet over moderate heat, until crispy.

3. Drain the bacon fat from the skillet and return to the heat.

4. Then, add the cream, Parmesan, and parsley to the skillet and stir to combine.

5. Drain the cooked tortellini, then add to the skillet, stir gently to coat the pasta in the sauce.

6. Serve straight away.

Tuna Pasta Bake

It is amazing just how many dishes you can make using canned goods as this cheesy fish pasta bake proves.

Servings: 6

Total Time: 35mins

Ingredients:

- 1 pound 7 ounces penne pasta
- 1¾ ounces butter
- 1¾ ounces plain flour
- 2½ cups milk
- 8¾ ounces Cheddar cheese (grated)
- 2 (4¼ ounces) cans tuna steak in spring water (undrained)
- 1 (11 ounces) can sweet corn (drained)
- A large handful of flat-leaf parsley (chopped)
- Salt and black pepper
- A large handful of Parmesan cheese (freshly grated)

Directions:

1. Preheat the main oven to 350 degrees F.

2. In a pan, cook the pasta in boiling salted water for 1-2 minutes less than the package directions.

3. In a second pan, melt the butter, cooking while vigorously stirring for 60 seconds.

4. Next, a little at a time, stir in the flour to create a white, thick consistency sauce.

5. Remove the pan from the heat. Then, stir in the grated cheese.

6. Drain the pasta and combine with the white sauce followed by the tuna, sweet corn, and parsley until incorporated—season to taste.

7. Next, transfer the mixture to a casserole dish and scatter with grated cheese.

8. Bake in the oven for 15-20 minutes until the cheese is crisp and golden.

Whole Wheat Pasta Chicken Caesar Salad

A pasta-salad hybrid is a perfect choice for those warmer days when you're hungry but don't feel like a hot meal.

Servings: 6

Total Time: 30mins

Ingredients:

- 8 ounces uncooked whole-wheat fusilli pasta
- 3 cups rotisserie chicken (shredded)
- 6 cups romaine lettuce (torn)
- 2 tomatoes (chopped)
- ½ cup Parmesan cheese (shredded)
- ½ cup store-bought Caesar dressing
- ⅓ cup toasted almond flakes

Directions:

1. Cook the fusilli using packet instructions. Drain. Then, rinse in cold water until cool.

2. Add the cool pasta to a large salad bowl along with the chicken, lettuce, tomatoes, and Parmesan cheese. Toss to combine.

3. Drizzle over the Caesar dressing and toss to coat.

4. Garnish the salad with toasted almond flakes and serve straight away.

Potato Dishes

Curried Beef and Instant Potato Bake

Make more of that package of instant mash lurking in the back of the cupboard and whip up a tasty curried beef dish for two.

Servings: 2

Total Time: 45mins

Ingredients:

- 2 tbsp oil
- 10 ounces minced beef
- 4 spring onions (sliced)
- 4 medium-size tomatoes (diced)
- Salt and freshly ground black pepper
- 2 tsp curry powder
- 2 cups water
- 2 packs instant potato flakes
- 4¼ tbsp Gouda cheese (grated)

Directions:

1. In a frying pan, heat the oil.

2. Add the minced beef and sauté until browned.

3. Next, add the spring onions followed by the tomatoes and simmer for approximately 20 minutes. Season with salt and black pepper. Stir in the curry powder.

4. Then, add 2 cups of water to the pan, stir well and remove from the heat.

5. Make up the instant mash as directed on the package instructions.

6. Lastly, transfer the beef mixture to a baking dish, top with the instant mash, scatter over the grated cheese and bake in the oven on moderate heat until golden brown. This will take 10-12 minutes.

Instant Mashed Potato Gnocchi

If you thought instant mash was a last resort, then think again, it's a versatile pantry staple that can be transformed into all number of great meals, including homemade gnocchi.

Servings: 4

Total Time: 25mins

Ingredients:

- 1 cup made-up instant mashed potato flakes
- 1 cup boiling water
- 1 egg (lightly beaten)
- 1½ cups flour
- ½ tsp dried basil
- ¼ tsp garlic powder
- ⅛ tsp salt
- ⅛ tsp black pepper
- 6 cups water
- Pasta sauce (store-bought, of choice, heated)
- Parmesan cheese (freshly grated, optional)

Directions:

1. Add the instant mash to a bowl.

2. Stir in the boiling water and add the beaten egg.

3. Stir in the flour along with the basil, garlic powder, salt, and black pepper.

4. Next, on a clean, lightly floured work surface, knead the mixture 10-12 times to create soft dough.

5. Divide the dough into 4 evenly-sized portions.

6. Next, on a clean, lightly floured work surface, roll each portion into a rope of no more than ½ "thick. Cut the rope into ¾"pieces. Press and gently roll each rope using a lightly floured fork.

7. In a pan, bring water to boil.

8. In batches, lower the gnocchi into the boiling water for 30-60 seconds, until they rise to the surface and float.

9. Using a slotted spoon remove from the water.

10. Serve the gnocchi with the sauce and garnish with grated Parmesan.

Mexican Hash Brown and Chicken Bake

Self-quarantine needn't mean lackluster family meals, and this Mexican-inspired hash brown with chicken recipe is proof positive that basic needn't mean boring. Top with fresh veggies and enjoy.

Servings: 4

Total Time: 35mins

Ingredients:

- 1 pound 2 ounces frozen hash browns
- 2 pounds 2 ounces chicken thigh fillets (trimmed and halved)
- 1 (1¼ ounces) sachet taco, fajita, or burrito seasoning
- 2 tbsp olive oil
- 1 large onion (peeled and coarsely chopped)
- 1 red capsicum (thinly sliced)
- 1 green capsicum (thinly sliced)

To Serve:

- Tomatoes (chopped)
- Cucumber (diced)
- Fresh parsley (chopped)

Directions:

1. In a single layer, microwave the hash brown for approximately 4-5 minutes. Break the hash browns into large-size pieces.

2. Toss the chicken with the seasoning and olive oil in a large-size roasting pan.

3. Add the onion along with the capsicums and toss thoroughly. Re-arrange the mixture, so it's in an even layer and top with the hash browns.

4. Cook at 430 degrees F for approximately 30 minutes until the chicken is sufficiently cooked through, and the hash browns are crisp.

5. Serve garnished with tomato, cucumber, and chopped parsley.

Parsley, Pesto, and Potato Pizzas

When drive-thru isn't an option, and you are craving a pizza but don't have lots of ingredients, then this potato pizza recipe is the way to go.

Servings: 4 (8") pizzas

Total Time: 1hour

Ingredients:

- 1 pound red potatoes (cut into ⅓" thick slices)
- Oil (to grease)
- Salt and freshly ground black pepper
- 1 cup flat-leaf parsley
- 2 tbsp walnuts (chopped)
- 1 clove of garlic (peeled and minced)
- ½ cup extra-virgin olive oil
- 2 (16 ounces) bags store-bought pizza dough
- ¾ cup fontina cheese (shredded)
- ¼ cup Parmesan cheese (grated)

Directions:

1. First, place a pizza stone on the oven rack in the bottom third of your oven. Arrange a second rack in the top third.

2. Preheat your main oven to 400 degrees F and preheat for 45-55 minutes to allow the pizza stone to heat.

3. In a single layer, arrange the sliced potatoes on a lightly oiled baking sheet. Season with salt and black pepper and bake in the top third of your oven for half an hour, until fork-tender.

4. Add the parsley, walnuts, garlic along with ½ teaspoon of salt to a food processor and pulse until finely chopped. While the food processor is still running, in a slow stream pour in the olive oil until smooth.

5. Next, turn the oven temperature up to 500 degrees F.

6. Roll out a ¼ of the dough into an 8" circle.

7. Then, put the dough on a floured pizza peel, arrange ¼ of the potatoes on top, allowing a ½" border all the way around.

8. Drizzle with ¼ of the pesto and scatter over ¼ of the cheese.

9. Slide the pizza onto the stone and bake for approximately 7-8 minutes, until the crust is golden and the cheese bubbles.

10. Repeat then the process with the remaining ingredients until all 4 pizzas are cooked.

11. Serve and enjoy.

Pecan-Topped Sweet Potato Bake

Sweet potatoes are highly nutritious. They are actually a great source of vitamins, minerals, and fiber, which makes them ideal for anyone concerned about staying healthy. This main is inexpensive and will feed a large-size family.

Servings: 6-8

Total Time: 45mins

Ingredients:

- 3 cups sweet potatoes (cooked and mashed)
- 2 eggs
- ½ cup sugar
- ¼ cup half-and-half cream
- ¼ cup butter (softened)
- 2 tsp vanilla extract
- ⅛ tsp salt

Topping:

- ½ cup packed brown sugar
- 2 tbsp all-purpose flour
- ¼ cup butter (cold, cut into cubes)
- ½ cup pecans (chopped)

Directions:

1. In a large-size bowl, combine the sweet potato mash with the eggs, sugar, half and half, butter, vanilla extract, and salt. Beat well until light and fluffy. Transfer the mixture to an 11x7" casserole dish.

2. For the topping, combine the brown sugar with the flour in a bowl. Cut in the cubed butter until a crumbly consistency.

3. Fold in the chopped pecans and sprinkle the mixture over the sweet potato mixture.

4. Then, bake at 350 degrees F, uncovered, for 30-35 minutes, or until the dish registers 160 degrees F.

5. Enjoy.

Potato and Ham Skillet

When you are staying home or self-quarantining, it's useful to have easy to make recipes on hand that use basic yet wholesome ingredients. This Potato and Ham skillet will tick that all-important box.

Servings: 4

Total Time: 20mins

Ingredients:

- 4 cups potatoes (peeled, cubed and cooked)
- 2 cups fully-cooked ham (cut into cubes)
- ½ cup mayonnaise
- ¼ tsp salt
- ⅛ tsp freshly ground black pepper
- 2 cups part-skim mozzarella cheese (shredded)

Directions:

1. In a large-size skillet, combine the cooked cubes of potatoes with the ham and mayonnaise. Then, season the mixture with salt and black pepper.

2. Cook while stirring over moderate-low heat, until sufficiently cooked through.

3. Stir in the shredded cheese until melted. Serve.

Potato, Pear, and Bacon Casserole

This casserole does have a lot of ingredients, but the good news is, they are all basic pantry staples, and this hearty, healthy casserole is well worth the effort.

Servings: 4

Total Time: 1hour 40mins

Ingredients:

- 1⅔ pounds potatoes (peeled and chopped)
- 1 tbsp sunflower oil
- 1 onion (peeled and diced)
- 1⅔ cups water
- Salt and black pepper
- 4 tbsp fresh thyme leaves (chopped)
- 2 ripe pears (sliced and cored)
- 1¼ pounds green beans (trimmed and halved)
- ⅔ cup milk
- 2 tbsp butter
- Pinch of grated nutmeg
- 3 tbsp fresh parsley (chopped)
- ⅔ cup vegetable stock
- 8¾ ounces bacon slices

Directions:

1. In a large-size pan of boiling, salted water cook the potatoes for 20 minutes.

2. In the meantime, in a large frying pan and heat the oil. Add the onions to the pan, then sauté for 5-6 minutes.

3. Deglaze the pan with the water, bring to boil and season.

4. Add the thyme to the pan, cover with a lid, and simmer for 10 minutes.

5. Preheat the main oven to 400 degrees F.

6. Add the pears along with the beans to the pan and simmer for 7-10 minutes.

7. In the meantime, drain the potatoes and with a potato masher, mash with the milk, butter, and a pinch of grated nutmeg.

8. Spoon the mash into a casserole dish.

9. Mix the chopped parsley into the veggies. With your slotted spoon, transfer them to the baking dish, arranging them evenly over the potatoes.

10. Pour the stock over the top, followed by the bacon.

11. Bake in the oven for 30-40 minutes, or until the bacon is crispy.

Slow Cooker Baked Potato Casserole

The potato may be humble, but it is also a very versatile food staple. So, if you want to limit any visits to the store, then this potato casserole using store cupboard staples is the one for you.

Servings: 8

Total Time: 5hours 35mins

Ingredients:

- 2½ pounds russet potatoes (peeled and diced into 1" cubes)
- 1 chicken bouillon cube
- Water (as needed)
- ¼ cup salted butter (melted)
- ½ tsp salt
- Dash of pepper
- Dash of onion powder
- 8 ounces sour cream
- 1 cup Cheddar cheese (divided)
- 8 ounces bacon (cooked, crumbled and divided)
- ½ bunch green onions (sliced and divided)

Directions:

1. Add the diced potatoes to a slow cooker of 4-quart capacity.

2. Add the chicken bouillon cubes along with sufficient water to cover entirely

3. On high, cook for 5 hours. Do not open the slow cooker lid during the cooking process.

4. When 5 hours have elapsed, drain the water off, and allow the potatoes to remain in the slow cooker.

5. Next, pour the melted butter evenly over the potatoes, season with salt, black pepper, and onion powder. With a potato masher, mash then the potatoes until you achieve your preferred consistency.

6. Pour in the sour cream followed by ½ cup of Cheddar cheese, 4 ounces of crumbled bacon, and half of the sliced green onion. Stir to combine.

7. Scatter the remaining Cheddar cheese over the top and replace the slow cooker lid. Continue cooking on high for an additional 20 minutes.

8. Garnish with the remaining bacon and onions and enjoy.

Spanish Potato Omelet

This Spanish tortilla can be enjoyed either chilled or warm. The fried potatoes and eggs are basic food staples making this main practicable and kind on the pocket. Serve with a green salad.

Servings: 8-10

Total Time: 40mins

Ingredients:

- ½ cup olive oil
- 5 potatoes (diced into 1" pieces)
- 1 large brown onion (peeled and chopped)
- 8 medium eggs
- Salt and black pepper
- Parsley (chopped, to garnish
- Green salad (to serve, optional)

Directions:

1. In a 12" nonstick frying pan, heat the olive oil.

2. Next, add the diced potatoes to the pan and fry until golden, crisp, and fork-tender.

3. Add the onion to the pan and fry until transparent. Using a metal colander, drain away all of the oil.

4. Return the veggies to the pan, re-arranging them into a single layer. Turn the heat down to low.

5. Then, in a bowl, beat the eggs with the salt and black pepper seasoning.

6. Pour the seasoned eggs into the frying pan, using a plastic spatula to gently move the veggie mixture around the eggs. Every now and again, carefully move the eggs around the potatoes around the pan while they cook to make sure that the eggs are cooking on the bottom.

7. Put a large dinner plate on top of the frying pan, and carefully invert the omelet onto the plate.

8. Slide the tortilla along with the onion and potatoes back into the pan,

9. Continue to cook, while occasionally and gently shaking the frying pan until the omelet is sufficiently cooked through.

10. Remove from the pan. Then, garnish with chopped parsley.

11. Serve and enjoy with a green salad.

Sweet Potato and Kale Chili

This flavorful and colorful chili will satisfy those spicy food cravings. In fact, even non-veggies will find this frugal dish so satisfying that they won't miss the meat.

Servings: 4

Total Time: 45mins

Ingredients:

- 1 tbsp olive oil
- 2 medium sweet potatoes (peeled, then chopped into 1" cubes)
- 1 clove of garlic (peeled and minced)
- 1 medium onion (peeled and diced)
- 1 red chili (finely chopped)
- ½ tsp cayenne pepper
- ½ tsp ground cinnamon
- ½ tsp ground cumin
- 1 (14½ ounces) can kidney beans (drained, then rinsed)
- 1 (14½ ounces) can chopped tomatoes
- 2 large handfuls kale
- Salt and black pepper

Directions:

1. In a large-size pan, heat the oil.

2. Next, add the potatoes to the pan along with the onion and garlic. Cook on moderate heat for 4-5 minutes, until the veggies soften slightly.

3. Stir in the red chili followed by the cayenne pepper, cinnamon, and cumin and continue cooking for an additional 2-3 minutes.

4. Next, add the beans and chopped tomatoes and stir to coat the veggies evenly and thoroughly. Simmer gently for approximately 30-35 minutes. Maybe, you need to add a drop of water to thin out the mixture's consistency.

5. Around 1 minute before the chili is cooked, add the kale and cook until it wilts slightly.

6. Season and serve.

Pulse Grain Dishes

Ancient Grain Beef Stew

Substitute red lentils and quinoa for potatoes and make this hearty, healthy, veggie-packed beef stew. It's fresh, filling, and fit for a family!

Servings: 8-10

Total Time: 8hours 30mins

Ingredients:

- 2 tbsp olive oil
- 1 pound beef stew meat (cut into 1" cubes)
- 4 celery ribs with leaves (chopped)
- 2 carrots (peeled and chopped)
- 1 large onion (peeled and chopped)
- 1½ cups dried lentils (rinsed)
- ½ cup red quinoa (rinsed)
- 5 large bay leaves
- 2 tsp ground cumin
- 1½ tsp salt
- 1 tsp dried tarragon
- ½ tsp black pepper
- 2 (32 ounces) cartons beef stock

Directions:

1. Over moderate heat, in a large-size frying pan or skillet, heat the oil.

2. Add the beef to the pan and brown all over.

3. Transfer the beef along with the drippings to a slow cooker of 5-6 quart capacity.

4. Stir in the remaining ingredients (celery ribs, carrots, onion, lentils, red quinoa, bay leaves, ground cumin, salt, tarragon, black pepper, and beef stock). Stir to combine.

5. Cook, while covered on low until the beef is tender, for 6-8 hours.

6. Remove and discard the bay leaf.

Broccoli Quinoa Skillet with Cheese and White Beans

Keeping healthy is a great way to fight colds, flu, and viruses, and this tasty dish featuring ancient grains is one of the best ways to ensure that you and your family enjoy the best nature has to offer.

Servings: 3-4

Total Time: 35mins

Ingredients:

- 1 tbsp extra-virgin olive oil
- 1 shallot (finely chopped)
- 4 cups fresh broccoli florets (chopped)
- 3 garlic cloves (peeled and minced)
- ¼ tsp sea salt
- ¼ tsp freshly ground black pepper
- ¾ cup uncooked quinoa
- 1½ cups low-sodium chicken stock
- 1 (14 ½ ounces) can low-salt white beans
- ¼ cup Parmesan cheese (freshly grated)
- 3 tbsp fresh parsley (chopped)

Directions:

1. Over moderately low heat, heat a large, deep-sided frying pan or skillet.

2. Add ½ tablespoon of oil to the pan and add the shallot. Cook until just softened, for approximately 2 minutes. Do not allow the shallot to brown.

3. Next, add the broccoli florets followed by the garlic, sea salt, and black pepper. Sauté until the florets are crisp-tender, for another 3-4 minutes. Take the broccoli and shallots out of the skillet and put to one side.

4. Add the remaining ½ tablespoon of oil to the pan.

5. Next, add the quinoa and allow to toast for 60 seconds while stirring frequently and scraping up the bits from the bottom of your pan.

6. Pour in the chicken stock and bring to boil before lowering the heat.

7. Then, cover your pan with a lid and allow to simmer for approximately 12 minutes, or until the quinoa is tender.

8. Add the white beans and broccoli florets set aside earlier and cook for 2 minutes until warmed through.

9. Stir in the grated cheese and scatter over the parsley.

10. Taste, season, and serve.

Chickpea Chicken with Curry Roasted Squash

If your family is self-isolating, then chickpeas, beans, lentils, and other pulses are a great source of fiber, protein, vitamins, and minerals for you and your family.

Servings: 8

Total Time: 50mins

Ingredients:

- 1 butternut squash (into ¾ "cubes)
- 1 red onion (peeled and chopped)
- 2 tbsp olive oil (divided)
- 2 tsp curry powder
- 1 tsp salt
- ¾ tsp black pepper
- 1½ cups water
- 1½ cups uncooked whole-wheat couscous
- 1 (14½ ounces) can reduced-sodium chicken broth
- ¾ cup dried apricots (coarsely chopped and divided)
- 3 cups rotisserie or leftover chicken (coarsely shredded)
- 1 (15 ounces) can chickpeas (rinsed, then drained)
- Fresh cilantro (minced)

Directions:

1. First, preheat the main oven to 425 degrees F.

2. Arrange the squash along with the red onion in a 15x10x1" baking pan.

3. Next, drizzle over 1 tablespoon of olive oil and scatter over with curry powder followed by ½ teaspoon of salt and ½ teaspoon of black pepper. Toss to coat evenly.

4. Then, roast in the oven for 25-30 minutes, until the squash is just tender, stirring the mixture halfway through roasting.

5. In a pan, bring the water and the remaining olive oil to boil.

6. Stir in the couscous and remove the pan from the heat. Allow to stand, while covered, for approximately 5 minutes, until the water is absorbed. Using a metal fork, fluff up the couscous.

7. In the meantime, in a stockpot of 6-quart capacity, combine the broth along with ½ cup of dried apricots, and bring to simmer.

8. Add the chicken, chickpeas and squash mixture along with the remaining seasoning, and while stirring gently, heat through.

9. Serve the curry with the couscous.

10. Scatter the remaining dried apricots over the top and garnish with minced cilantro.

Greek-Style Savory Oatmeal

Oatmeal isn't just a sweet breakfast dish; it can also be the main ingredient for an evening meal too. This Greek-inspired oatmeal features easy-to-source ingredients and top with whatever you have to hand.

Servings: 2

Total Time: 20mins

Ingredients:

- ¼ cup red onion (peeled and diced)
- Olive oil
- ½ cup water
- 1 cup unsweetened soy milk
- ½ cup quick-cook steel cut oats
- 1 cup zucchini (grated)
- 4 tbsp store-bought hummus
- Salt and freshly ground black pepper
- Handful of spinach (cut into strips)

Optional Toppings:

- Kalamata olives (pitted and halved)
- Sun-dried tomatoes
- Feta cheese (crumbled)
- Pine nuts (toasted)
- Fresh parsley (chopped)

Directions:

1. In a frying pan, sauté the red onion in a splash of olive oil until translucent.

2. Pour in the water and milk and bring to boil.

3. Next, stir in the oats along, followed by the zucchini. Reduce the heat to medium.

4. Once most of the liquid is absorbed fold in the hummus and season with salt and black pepper.

5. When the oatmeal is your desired consistency, turn off the heat. Next, add the spinach while stirring to incorporate.

6. Then, divide the mixture between 2 bowls and top with olives, sun-dried tomatoes, Feta cheese crumbles, and toasted pine nuts.

7. Garnish with fresh parsley and serve.

Lentil Stew

This comforting meat-free stew has amazing taste and texture. Better yet, you can adjust the seasonings and add extra veggies if needed.

Servings: 6-8

Total Time: 25mins

Ingredients:

- 6 tbsp olive oil
- 4 carrots
- 2 yellow onions (peeled and diced)
- 4 celery stalks (diced)
- 6 garlic cloves (peeled and finely chopped)
- 2 tbsp balsamic vinegar
- 4 tbsp paprika
- ½ tsp cayenne pepper
- ½ tsp ground cumin
- 2½ cups red lentils (rinsed)
- 8 cups vegetable stock
- Salt and black pepper
- 4 tbsp freshly squeezed lemon juice

Directions:

1. First, in your Dutch oven or large pot, heat the oil over moderate heat.

2. Add the carrots, onion, and celery and stir for 5-6 minutes or until the onions are translucent.

3. Toss in the chopped garlic and stir until fragrant. Add the balsamic vinegar followed by the paprika, cayenne pepper, cumin, and red lentils. Stir thoroughly to combine.

4. Pour in the stock and season with salt and black pepper. Stir well and bring it to simmer.

5. Partially cover the pot and allow the stew to simmer for approximately 8-10 minutes.

6. Stir in the freshly squeezed lemon juice and serve.

Roasted Garlic Bulgar Burgers

Now you actually have more time on your hands, and cooking can become a pleasure rather than a chore, these homemade, meat-free burgers are well worth the effort. Bulgar has more fiber than oats, millet, and quinoa and is perfectly combined with tart dried cherries and chopped walnuts.

Servings: 4

Total Time: 9hours 20mins

Ingredients:

- 1 head of garlic
- 1 tsp extra-virgin olive oil
- 1 (6") sprig of rosemary (leaves stripped)
- 1 cup quick-cook bulgur
- 2 cups water
- ¼ cup walnuts (chopped)
- Nonstick cooking spray
- ¼ pound spinach (cleaned and dried)
- ½ cup dried cherries
- 4 burger buns (split)
- Dill pickles or mustard (to serve, optional)

Directions:

1. First, roast the garlic. Then, preheat the main oven to 350 degrees F.

2. In the meantime, trim ¼" off the top of the head of garlic to reveal the cloves. Set in a small piece of foil, drizzle with olive oil and wrap tightly—Bake in the oven for 45 minutes before opening the foil and allowing it to cool.

3. In the meantime, add the rosemary leaves, quick-cook bulgur, and water and to a small pan over moderate heat. Bring to boil, and reduce to low heat, cover with a lid and allow to cook for 15 minutes.

4. Remove the pan from the heat pour off the extra water and allow it to cool.

5. In a small, dry frying pan, over moderate heat toast the walnuts for 2-3 minutes, until they emit their fragrance. Remove from the pan, then put to one side.

6. Using the same pan, coat with nonstick cooking spray and add the spinach. Remove then the pan from the heat and, if watery, drain.

7. Once the garlic and bulgur are cooked, transfer all of the mixtures, including the dried cherries, to a food processor. Process until silky smooth or on pulse, process until chunky.

8. Transfer to the fridge overnight. Doing this will help to make the mixture easier to work with.

9. The following day, when you are ready to serve, evenly divide the mixture into 4 even-size patties and over moderate heat in a pan brown on both sides.

10. Add the burgers to the buns along with dill pickles or a dollop of mustard.

Slow Cooker Chicken and Pinto Bean Soup

These days, wasting food isn't an option, so if you are looking for ways to use up leftover chicken, this hearty bean soup is ideal.

Servings: 4-6

Total Time: 7hours 20mins

Ingredients:

- 1 bag dried pinto beans
- 1 yellow onion (peeled and diced)
- 8 white mushrooms (sliced)
- 1 cup cooked, leftover chicken (diced)
- 1 tbsp kosher salt
- 1 tsp freshly ground black pepper
- 1 tbsp Italian seasoning
- 1 cup water
- 4 cups chicken stock
- Large handful of fresh baby spinach
- French bread (to serve, optional)

Directions:

1. Add the pinto beans to a large pan. Fill the pan with sufficient water to cover the beans by 2".

2. Next, bring to boil before reducing to a simmer and allowing to cook, uncovered, for 10 minutes.

3. Then, remove your pan from the heat, cover with a lid, and allow to sit for 60 minutes. Drain well.

4. Add the pinto beans along with the onion, mushrooms, cooked chicken, kosher salt, black pepper and Italian seasoning, water, and chicken stock to your slow cooker.

5. On high, cook for 6 hours.

6. Add the spinach and continue to cook for 1-2 hours or until the pinto beans are bite tender.

7. Lastly, serve with French bread to mop up the soup.

Stovetop Vegan Mac 'n Cheese

This super creamy iconic dish with cannellini beans is quick to prepare and perfect for anyone who isn't a big fan of cheese.

Servings: 4-6

Total Time: 2hours 20mins

Ingredients:

- 3 ounces raw cashews (soaked in water overnight and drained)
- ½ cup cannellini beans (cooked)
- ½ tsp smoked paprika
- 2 tbsp freshly squeezed lemon juice
- 1 tsp ground turmeric
- ¼ cup nutritional yeast
- 2 tbsp white miso
- 1 small-size clove of garlic (peeled and crushed)
- Dash of cayenne pepper
- ½ cup water
- 12 ounces whole-wheat elbow pasta
- Salt (to season)
- 1 cup green veggies (of choice, to serve)

Directions:

1. Add the cashews, cooked cannellini beans, smoked paprika, fresh lemon juice, turmeric, nutritional yeast, miso, garlic, cayenne pepper, and water into a food blender or processor and process until silky smooth. Put the sauce to one side.

2. Second, bring a pan of salted water to boil and add whole wheat pasta. Cook according to the package directions, and until al dente. Drain thoroughly and return to the pan: taste and season.

3. Add the cashew sauce and gently fold to combine and evenly coat the pasta.

4. Serve with your choice of green veggies and enjoy.

Three Bean Curry

You will be amazed at how a few canned store-cupboard staples along with a whole heap of spices can come together to create a spicy, pulse-packed curry.

Servings: 4

Total Time: 35mins

Ingredients:

- 1 tbsp oil
- ½ tsp cumin seeds
- 1 red onion (peeled and chopped)
- 1 green chili (chopped)
- Salt
- 1 tsp ginger (peeled and grated)
- 1 tsp garlic (peeled and grated)
- 1 (14 ounces) can fire-roasted diced tomatoes
- 1 tsp curry powder
- ¼ tsp turmeric
- ½ tsp cumin
- ¼ tsp garam masala
- ½ cup canned kidney beans (rinsed and drained)
- ½ cup canned white beans (rinsed and drained)
- ½ cup canned black beans (rinsed and drained)
- 1-1½ cups water
- ½ cup coconut milk
- 2 tbsp cilantro (chopped)
- Freshly squeezed juice of ½ lemon

Directions:

1. In a pan, heat the oil.

2. Once hot, add the cumin seeds along and toast until they make a crackling sound.

3. Add the onion, followed by the green chili. Sauté for a couple of minutes adding a pinch of salt to season while they fry.

4. Next, stir in the ginger and garlic and cook for 2-3 minutes.

5. Add the canned tomatoes, and cook, while stirring for 4-5 minutes.

6. Add a pinch more salt along with the curry powder, cumin, turmeric, garam masala, and stir to combine. Cook the spices with the tomatoes for another 3-4 minutes.

7. Stir in the kidney beans, white beans, and black beans. Cover with a lid and on moderate heat cook for 5 minutes.

8. Pour in 1 cup of water along with the coconut milk, stir well to combine, adding water if needed to adjust the consistency. Then, taste and season accordingly.

9. Allow the curry to simmer for an additional 5 minutes before adding the cilantro.

10. Add the lemon juice and serve.

Turkey and Vegetable Barley Soup

When you can't make lots of trips to the store, it's time to reach for the grains and pulses! And this chunky turkey and veggie barley soup is a great way to inject much-needed comfort and flavor into family mealtimes.

Servings: 6

Total Time: 20mins

Ingredients:

- 1 tbsp canola oil
- 5 carrots (chopped)
- 1 onion (chopped)
- ⅔ cup quick-cooking barley
- 6 cups reduced-sodium chicken broth
- 2 cups cooked turkey breast (cubed)
- 2 cups fresh baby spinach
- ½ tsp black pepper

Directions:

1. In your large pan, heat the oil over moderate to high heat.

2. Add the carrots and onion and cook, while stirring for 4-5 minutes, until the carrots are crisp-tender.

3. Stir in the barley along with the chicken broth and bring to boil.

4. Turn the heat down and simmer, while covered, until the carrots and barley are tender, for 10-12 minutes.

5. Stir in the turkey followed by the spinach and black pepper.

6. Heat the soup through and serve.

Rice Dishes

Baked Rice with Butternut Squash

A warming dish with a rich, comforting flavor is the perfect dinner to cozy up with.

Servings: 6

Total Time: 20mins

Ingredients:

- Nonstick cooking spray
- 1 butternut squash
- 1 cup water
- 2 cups chicken broth
- 1 tbsp fresh sage (chopped)*
- 1 tsp olive oil
- 1 cup yellow onion (diced)
- 2 cloves garlic (peeled and minced)
- 1 cup uncooked short-grain or Arborio rice
- ¼ cup dry white wine
- 1 tsp fresh thyme (chopped)**
- ½ tsp salt
- ¼ tsp black pepper
- ¼ cup Parmesan cheese (grated)

Directions:

1. First, preheat the main oven to 350 degrees F. Spritz a 9x13" baking dish with nonstick cooking spray.

2. Arrange the squash on a baking sheet, place in the oven, and bake for half an hour, until tender. Take out of your oven and allow to completely cool.

3. Peel the squash, half lengthwise, and discard the membranes and seeds. Cube the flesh.

4. Next, increase the oven temperature to 400 degrees F.

5. In a saucepan over moderate heat, bring the water, broth, and sage to a simmer.

6. Next, in the meantime, warm the oil in a skillet over moderately high heat. Add the onion and sauté for several minutes. Add the garlic, then sauté for 2 minutes.

7. Then, add the rice, stir, and continue to cook for 60 more seconds.

8. Add the diced squash to the skillet along with the white wine, thyme, salt, black pepper, and simmering broth mixture. Stir and cook for 5 minutes.

9. Lastly, transfer the mixture to the prepared baking dish and place in the hot oven— Bake for half an hour. Stir the mixture gently and then sprinkle over the Parmesan. Return to the oven for 5 minutes, until the cheese melts.

*Can substitute 1 tsp dried rubbed sage

**Can substitute ¼ tsp dried thyme

Beef and Sweet Pepper Skillet

This tasty skillet combines lean beef, wholesome brown rice, and sweet peppers for a dish that has both flavor and nutritional value. There's no need to pile on the pounds when self-isolating at home.

Servings: 6

Total Time: 35mins

Ingredients:

- 1 pound lean ground beef
- 1 (14½ ounces) can diced tomatoes with green chilies
- 1 tbsp chili powder
- 1 (14½ ounces) can beef broth
- ¼ tsp salt
- ⅛ tsp powdered garlic
- 2 cups instant brown rice
- 1 sweet red pepper (sliced thinly)
- 1 green pepper (sliced thinly)
- 1 cup Monterey Jack cheese (shredded)

Directions:

1. In your skillet over moderate heat, brown the beef for several minutes, stirring often. Drain away any fat from the skillet.

2. Add the canned tomatoes, chili powder, beef broth, salt, and powdered garlic.

3. Stir in the brown rice and peppers. Turn the heat down, then simmer for 8-10 minutes without a lid until the rice has absorbed the liquid.

4. Lastly, take the skillet off the heat and sprinkle over the Monterey Jack cheese. Cover with a lid and allow to stand for 2-3 minutes so the cheese can melt before serving.

Chicken and Wild Rice Soup

Dinner needn't always be super heavy and rich. Sometimes what you need is a light and wholesome option, especially if your gym visits have been canceled because of self-quarantining!

Servings: 4

Total Time: 30mins

Ingredients:

- 1 (6.2 ounces) packet long grain and wild rice
- 2 tbsp butter
- 1 rib celery (diced)
- 1 yellow onion (peeled and diced)
- 1 carrot (peeled, diced)
- 1 clove of garlic (peeled and minced)
- 2 tbsp all-purpose flour
- 3 cups skim milk
- 1½ cups chicken broth
- 2 cups cooked, cubed chicken

Directions:

1. Cook the rice using packet instructions.

2. Second, in the meantime, melt the butter in a large saucepan over moderate heat.

3. Add the celery, onion, and carrot, sauté for several minutes until tender.

4. Add the garlic and sauté for another 60 seconds.

5. Stir in the flour until well incorporated. While whisking the mixture, pour in the milk and chicken broth in steady streams.

6. Next, bring the soup to a boil while stirring continuously. Boil for 2-3 minutes until thickened.

7. Finally, stir in the cooked chicken and rice. Continue to cook until hot through before serving.

Rice Meatloaf

If you're bored of your regular meatloaf recipe and looking to take yours to the next level, then this recipe is for you! Adding rice to your meatloaf mixture gives a firm texture without drying it out, the result is a moist and juicy loaf.

Servings: 8

Total Time: 1hour 30mins

Ingredients:

- Butter (to grease)
- ½ cup uncooked instant white rice
- 1 pound lean ground beef
- ¼ cup red bell pepper (diced)
- ¼ cup yellow onion (diced)
- 1 garlic clove (peeled and minced)
- 1 tsp salt
- 1 tsp black pepper
- 2 tsp Worcestershire sauce
- 1 tbsp fresh mixed herbs (minced)
- 1 egg (beaten)
- ¼ cup tomato ketchup
- ¼ cup dry breadcrumbs
- ¼ cup skim milk

Directions:

1. First, preheat the main oven to 350 degrees F. Grease a small loaf tin with butter.

2. In your large bowl, combine the rice, beef, bell pepper, onion, garlic, salt, black pepper, Worcestershire sauce, mixed herbs, egg, tomato ketchup, breadcrumbs, and milk using clean hands.

3. Transfer the meat mixture to the loaf tin, don't pack down the mixture too tightly.

4. Next, place in the oven and bake for approximately an hour or until the meatloaf registers an internal temperature of 160 degrees F.

5. Lastly, take the meatloaf out of the oven and allow to rest for 10-15 minutes before slicing and serving.

Salmon Rice Puff

Canned salmon is an easy-to-source ingredient and, although relatively inexpensive, can be used in a variety of delicious recipes such as this salmon rice puff.

Servings: 3-4

Total Time: 35mins

Ingredients:

- Butter (to grease)
- ½ cup skim milk
- 2 eggs
- 1 cup cooked long-grain rice
- 1 (14¾ ounces) can salmon (drained, skins and bone removed)
- ¼ cup celery (chopped)
- ¼ cup scallions (chopped)
- ½ tsp Worcestershire sauce
- 4 tbsp fresh lemon juice
- ½ cup Cheddar cheese (shredded)

Directions:

1. First, preheat the main oven to 375 degrees F. Grease a 1½-quart baking dish with butter.

2. Second, whisk together the milk and eggs in a large bowl. Stir in the rice, salmon, celery, scallions, Worcestershire sauce, and lemon juice.

3. Transfer the mixture to the prepared baking dish. Place in the oven and bake for 20 minutes.

4. Next. sprinkle the cheese over the casserole and return to the oven for 10 more minutes until the cheese melts.

5. Lastly, take out of the oven and allow to stand for a few minutes before serving.

Seafood Casserole

Tender, juicy seafood combines with a silky white sauce to create an indulgent but easy-to-make casserole that is a real treat for all the family.

Servings: 6

Total Time: 1hour

Ingredients:

- Butter (to grease)

- 1 (6 ounces) packet wild rice

- 2½ cups canned lump crabmeat (drained)

- 2 ribs celery (chopped)

- 1 pound shrimp (cooked, peeled, and chopped)

- 1 yellow onion (peeled, diced)

- ½ cup bell pepper (diced)

- 1 (4 ounces) can mushrooms pieces and stems (drained)

- 1 (2 ounces) jar pimientos (drained, diced)

- ½ tsp black pepper

- 1 cup full-fat mayonnaise

- 1 cup skim milk

- ⅛ tsp Worcestershire sauce

- ¼ cup dry breadcrumbs

Directions:

1. First, preheat the main oven to 375 degrees F. Grease a 9x13" baking dish with butter.

2. Cook the rice using packet instructions.

3. In a bowl, combine the crabmeat, celery, shrimp, onion, bell pepper, mushrooms, and pimientos.

4. In a smaller bowl, stir together the black pepper, mayonnaise, skim milk, and Worcestershire sauce. Fold the sauce into the seafood mixture.

5. Next, fold in the cooked rice.

6. Then, transfer the mixture to the prepared baking dish. Scatter over the breadcrumbs.

7. Place the casserole in the oven, then bake for approximately 45 minutes or until the mixture is bubbling.

8. Allow to rest for 4-5 minutes before serving.

Slow-Cooked North African Chicken and Rice

Simply throw the ingredients into your slow cooker mid-afternoon, and come dinnertime, you'll be tucking into a sweet and spicy North African chicken and rice dish. Better yet, with little to no washing up, you'll have even more time to make the most out of being home with your family.

Servings: 8

Total Time: 5hours 10mins

Ingredients:

- 1 yellow onion (peeled and diced)
- 1 tbsp olive oil
- 2 pounds skinless, boneless chicken thighs
- 1 tsp paprika
- 1 tsp turmeric
- ½ tsp black pepper
- 1 tsp sea salt
- ½ tsp chili powder
- ½ tsp cinnamon
- 1 cup raisins
- ¾ cup pitted green olives (chopped)
- 1 lemon (sliced)
- 2 cloves of garlic (peeled and minced)
- 1 tbsp fresh cilantro (minced)
- ½ cup chicken broth
- 4 cups cooked brown rice (hot, to serve)

Directions:

1. In a 4-quart slow cooker, combine the diced onion and olive oil.

2. Arrange the chicken thighs over the onion.

3. In a small bowl, combine the paprika, turmeric, black pepper, sea salt, chili powder, and cinnamon. Sprinkle the spice mix over the chicken.

4. Scatter over the raisins, chopped olives, lemon slices, and minced garlic. Finally, sprinkle over the fresh cilantro. Pour over the chicken broth.

5. Cook for 4-5 hours on low heat until the chicken is cooked through and tender.

6. Serve with cooked brown rice.

South of the Border Pork Chops

If you're stuck at home all day, then a fun and delicious dinner is just what you need! These South of the Border pork chops are baked on top of rice and covered with melting cheese and bell peppers.

Servings: 6

Total Time: 1hour 15mins

Ingredients:

- Butter (to grease)
- 2 tbsp canola oil
- 6 pork loin chops
- Seasoned salt and black pepper
- 1 (8 ounces) can tomato sauce
- 1½ cups water
- ¾ cup uncooked long grain rice
- 2 tbsp taco seasoning
- 1 green bell pepper (deseeded, diced)
- ½ cup Cheddar cheese (shredded)

Directions:

1. First, preheat the main oven to 350 degrees F. Grease a 9x13" baking dish with butter.

2. Second, warm the oil in a skillet over moderately high heat,

3. Season the pork chops with salt and black pepper, add to the skillet and brown on both sides.

4. In the meantime, combine the tomato sauce, water, rice, and taco seasoning in the baking dish.

5. Next, arrange the browned chops on top of the rice mixture in the baking dish.

6. Scatter over the green bell pepper.

7. Then, cover the dish with kitchen foil and bake in the oven for an hour.

8. Uncover the dish, sprinkle over the shredded cheese, and return to the oven for 5 more minutes until the cheese melts.

9. Serve straight away.

Speedy Chicken Fried Rice

A delicious fried rice dish that's ready in less than 20 minutes? Who needs takeout!

Servings: 6

Total Time: 20mins

Ingredients:

- 12 ounces frozen mixed vegetables
- 2 tbsp olive oil
- 2 eggs (beaten)
- 4 tbsp sesame oil
- 3 (8 ounces) packages frozen ready-to-serve vegetable rice
- 1 rotisserie chicken (skin removed, shredded)
- ¼ tsp salt
- ¼ tsp black pepper

Directions:

1. Cook the frozen vegetables using packet instructions.

2. Second, warm 1 tablespoon of olive oil in a skillet over moderately high heat. Pour the eggs into the skillet and cook, while stirring, until just set. Tip the egg out of the pan into a bowl.

3. Using the same skillet, warm 2 tsp sesame oil, and remaining olive oil. Add the frozen rice and cook for 10-12 minutes until browned.

4. Add the shredded chicken, salt, and black pepper.

5. Return the eggs to the skillet along with the cooked frozen veggies. Stir to combine and cook until hot through.

6. Drizzle over the remaining sesame oil and serve.

Stuffed Peppers with Cheese and Tomato Sauce

This oven-baked main is perfect for all the family, thanks to perfectly-seasoned rice and beef filling and a cheese tomato sauce topping.

Servings: 8

Total Time: 1hour 15mins

Ingredients:

Peppers:

- 2 pounds ground beef
- 1 green bell pepper (seeded, chopped)
- 1 yellow onion (peeled and diced)
- 2 cloves of garlic (peeled and minced)
- 1 tsp salt
- ½ tsp black pepper
- 1 (10 ounces) can (optional flavor) diced tomatoes with green chilis
- 1 (14½ ounces) can diced tomatoes
- 1 (15 ounces) can tomato sauce
- 3¾ cups water
- 1 tbsp cumin
- 3 cups uncooked instant rice
- 4 large green bell peppers (deseeded, tops sliced off)

Sauce:

- 1½ pounds American cheese (cubed)
- 1 (10 ounces) can diced tomato with green chilis

Directions:

1. First, preheat the main oven to 350 degrees F.

2. Second, in a Dutch oven over moderate heat, sauté the beef, bell pepper, yellow onion, garlic, salt, and black pepper until the beef is browned all over. Drain away any fat from the skillet.

3. Add the canned tomatoes and tomato sauce, water, and cumin to the Dutch oven and bring to a boil. Turn the heat down to a simmer. Then, cook for 10 minutes uncovered.

4. Stir in the rice and simmer for another 5 minutes. Take off the heat, cover with a lid, and allow to stand for 5 minutes.

5. Slice the peppers in half widthwise and boil the pepper halves in water for 4 minutes. Drain the water from the peppers.

6. Stuff the pepper halves equally with the beef and rice mixture.

7. Arrange the stuffed peppers in a 9x13" baking dish. Cover with kitchen foil and bake for an hour.

8. Just before serving, combine the cubed cheese and canned tomatoes in a small pan over moderately high heat, stirring until the cheese melts.

9. Serve the sauce poured over the cooked stuffed peppers.

Author's Afterthoughts

I would like to express my deepest thanks to you, the reader, for making this investment in one my books. I cherish the thought of bringing the love of cooking into your home.

With so much choice out there, I am grateful you decided to Purch this book and read it from beginning to end.

Please let me know by submitting an Amazon review if you enjoyed this book and found it contained valuable information to help you in your culinary endeavors. Please take a few minutes to express your opinion freely and honestly. This will help others make an informed decision on purchasing and provide me with valuable feedback.

Thank you for taking the time to review!

Christina Tosch

About the Author

Christina Tosch is a successful chef and renowned cookbook author from Long Grove, Illinois. She majored in Liberal Arts at Trinity International University and decided to pursue her passion of cooking when she applied to the world renowned Le Cordon Bleu culinary school in Paris, France. The school was lucky to recognize the immense talent of this chef and she excelled in her courses, particularly Haute Cuisine. This skill was recognized and rewarded by several highly regarded Chicago restaurants, where she was offered the prestigious position of head chef.

Christina and her family live in a spacious home in the Chicago area and she loves to grow her own vegetables and herbs in the garden she lovingly cultivates on her sprawling estate. Her and her husband have two beautiful children, 3 cats, 2 dogs and a parakeet they call Jasper. When Christina is not hard at work creating beautiful meals for Chicago's elite, she is hard at work writing engaging e-books of which she has sold over 1500.

Make sure to keep an eye out for her latest books that offer helpful tips, clear instructions and witty anecdotes that will bring a smile to your face as you read!